# Historic Coffeehouses

*Vienna*

❖

*Budapest*

❖

*Prague*

by
## Carol Dittrich

Published by Lemieux International, Ltd.
P. O. Box 170134
Milwaukee, Wisconsin 53217
Cover design & photographs by Carol Dittrich
Graphics by Michael Olive @ Olive Art Studio
Manufactured in the United States of America

ISBN 0-9667269-9-5

Library of Congress Cataloging in Publication Data

Dittrich, Carol A. Date-
  Historic coffeehouses : Vienna, Budapest, Prague / by Carol
Dittrich
      p. cm
    ISBN 0-9667269-9-5
  1. Coffeehouses—Austria—Vienna—Guidebooks. 2.
Coffeehouses—Hungary—Budapest—Guidebooks. 3.
Coffeehouses—Czech Republic----Prague—Guidebooks. 4.
Coffeehouses—Austria—Vienna—History. 5.
Coffeehouses—Hungary—Budapest—History. 6.
Coffeehouses—Czech Republic—Prague—History. 1. Title.
  TX907.5.A82 V543 2002
  647.95'09436'13—dc21

                    2002001854

This book is dedicated
to the memory of my Mother
and her friends,
who introduced me to the
pleasure of drinking Turkish coffee
and the art of reading the cup.

# ACKNOWLEDGEMENTS

I extend my gratitude to my family, especially Buz and Terence, for their encouragement and support. A special acknowledgment and heartfelt thanks to my Hungarian, Austrian and Czech friends, and my cousin Katalin for assisting in the research for this book. I would also like to thank the proprietors and staff of the coffeehouses of Vienna, Budapest and Prague who were all most helpful at the time of my visits. I also extend a special thank you for the maps which were the work of Oscar Dittrich and Milwaukee Map.

# AUTHOR'S NOTE

As you embark on your adventure into the
world of the coffeehouse culture, you will discover
that the past blends with the present where dreams
are explored and formulated, where creativity is
nurtured and the intellect stimulated, where
generations share their wit and wisdom, while
lovers exchange intimate thoughts and promises.

Allow your imagination to flow freely as you
experience the many splendors of Vienna, Budapest
and Prague.

**Note:**

The words *coffeehouse* and *cafe* as used in this book are synonymous.

The author has enjoyed visiting the coffeehouses presented in this book, as I'm sure you will also. At the time of this writing, all of the information is correct. However, unforeseen conditions may result in unannounced closures or name changes, as well changes in hours of operation.

# CONTENTS

**INTRODUCTION**

# CONTENTS continued

## BUDAPEST

# CONTENTS continued

## PRAGUE

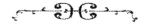

# INTRODUCTION

"Coffee, must be hot as hell, black as the devil
pure as an angel, and sweet as love."
A Turkish saying

Kaffee, Kave, Kava, Coffee. However it is pronounced, coffee speaks eloquently to the palate, is universally appealing and democratic in its consumption. Coffee is classic, calming and stimulating. It is an experience that invites you to embrace a moment of solitude or socialize with others. A symbol of hospitality throughout most of the world, a cup of coffee can soothe the soul, or perhaps even predict your future.

The origins of coffee remain hidden among the mysteries of the East, shrouded in oriental tales and legend. The generally accepted explanation is that human cultivation of the coffee plant first developed on the continent of Africa or Arabia, either in Ethiopia or

Yemen. The introduction of coffee as a beverage appears to be legendary. It is believed that the coffee drink was used for medicinal purposes by the Arabians as early as the 6th century.

The introduction of coffee consumption into the Middle East appears to have occurred during the latter part of the fifteenth century. It was first used by the Sufi mystical religious order who were seeking a substitute for wine, which was forbidden by the Islamic Koran. Coffee provided an acceptable beverage for their devotional rituals and a stimulant which would keep them awake for all-night religious ceremonies. The drink was called *bunchum* from the plant *bunn*, and was made from the hull and the pulp surrounding the bean itself. After boiling the toasted hull, a sweet and caffinated beverage was produced.

While coffee remained an important aspect of the Sufi religious ritual, the purpose of the drink and its use began to change. The Syrians as well as the secular society discovered the benefit of roasting the seeds of the coffee bean and began cultivating the drinking of coffee as a social experience in a comfortable venue. It was not long before roasted coffee and its consumption reached across the Muslim world, arriving in Istanbul (Constantinople) Turkey by mid sixteenth century.

The first coffeehouses appeared in Mecca where a coffeehouse lifestyle was created, an atmosphere filled with stimulating discussions and delicious thirst-quenching coffee. At first coffeehouses were not well received by the government because they felt that gatherings could incite dissent against the authority. But once the ruling power realized that coffeehouses were an important source of tax revenue, the persecution of the coffeehouse owners ceased. The coffeehouse culture flourished and began to spread eastward.

The coffeehouses or *cafenets* of the East, centered primarily in Constantinople and Damascus, were usually scattered about in spaces that provided a view of the square, not to mention refuge from a scorching desert sun. Since women stayed home, the cafe was the domain of men. Both young and old sat, drank coffee and contemplated life while smoking sweet-smelling tobacco from water pipes called houkas. Being a center for passive activity, patrons would spend hours playing backgammon, chess or cards. One of the favorite card games was bridge, and it is believed that the game probably originated in the *cafenets* of Constantinople.

As the popularity of the coffee drink continued to expand, it became an important aspect of everyday life. Coffee was no longer consumed within a distinct coffeehouse ritual, nor did it remain exclusive to the coffeehouses. The use of coffee became the symbol of hospitality in the home, where coffee beans were ground to a powdery consistency with a hand grinder, brewed, and served in a demitasse type cup. If desired, an accent of sugar was added to disguise its bitterness to the palate. All levels of society embraced the ritual of preparing and serving coffee in the home, whether for entertaining the customer, for business purposes, or for an elaborate ceremony with invited guests.

The Ottoman Turks were the main facilitators of introducing coffee drinking to the rest of the world, including continental Europe. As a result of their expanding empire, commercial and cultural exchanges developed with England and the Netherlands via Italy and the sea. After penetration of the Balkans they spread up to the gates of Vienna and eventually Central Europe. Thus the term "Turkish coffee".

When the coffeehouses were opened in Europe after 1645, they were run mostly by foreigners from the Middle-East and the Balkans, who were familiar with the trade. The owners attempted to replicate the surroundings of the original Middle East coffeehouses, offering an exclusively male meeting place. Men could congregate and pass the time with many of the same activities practiced by their counterparts while drinking Turkish coffee. At the same time, many existing traditional taverns refurbished their interiors and added coffee to their service to conform to the new coffeehouse trend. As coffeehouses became more established within European cultures, their style began to change, expanding into cafes serving food and confection.

In 1652, a Greek, Pasqua Rosée, established the first coffeehouse in London, the business center of the world. Eventually the idea spread through Great Britain and across to Amsterdam. French merchants from Marseilles, who had acquired the coffee habit during their travels along the Mediterranean Sea, sensed a good business opportunity. They began importing coffee from Egypt and the Middle East. To capitalize on the mysterious beverage they opened a coffeehouse in Marseilles in 1671. An Armenian by the name of Pascal served coffee for the first time in a Paris cafe in 1672. Once started, the momentum of the coffeehouse's popularity continued, reaching Germany and its major cities, Bremen, Hamburg and Leipzig by the turn of the century.

Foreign coffeehouse owners continued to establish themselves in other cities of Europe. After an

Armenian merchant named Diodato opened a coffeehouse in Vienna in 1685, coffeehouses proliferated. Uniquely, the Viennese coffeehouse had a certain style and appeal which reached beyond Vienna and its environs.

Gorgos Hatalah II Damaski, otherwise known as Jiri Deodatus, The Wandering Turk, opened the first coffeehouse in Prague in 1708 under the sign, The Golden Serpent.

Influenced by the Ottomans, the coffeehouse in Budapest was present long before the habit of coffee drinking reached either Vienna or Paris. The 150-year Turkish occupation (1541-1686) had brought with it coffee and the coffeehouses, which were characteristically Turkish. However, it was not until 1714 that a gentleman known as Blasius opened what is considered the first uniquely Hungarian coffeehouse in Buda.

The venue of the coffeehouse and the mysteries of Turkish coffee changed at the beginning of the 18th century when women fortune-tellers began to prophesy the future of an individual by interpreting the coffee grounds left in the cup of the drinker. It was a spiritual journey into the future and the foretelling of one's fate. The art of "reading the cup" remains popular throughout Europe and the Middle East.

The golden age of the coffeehouse reached its height at the end of the opulent 19th century when they flourished throughout the Austro-Hungarian Empire. While coffeehouses of the various nations may have differed in ambiance and style, they all shared the same coffeehouse spirit. It is a culture that remains even today. They were centers for political, literary and artistic influence, a venue where sages shared their wisdom and great ideas were born. They were also a place with an atmosphere of intimate conversations and lovers' promises.

As a result of economic, social and political changes, the number of coffeehouses declined after World War II. It was no longer profitable to have the patrons linger for hours over a cup of coffee, nor did the younger generation have an interest in a social experience that was considered establishment. Budapest and Prague, under the siege of the Communist regime, witnessed the closure of many of their coffeehouses, which the Communists viewed as potential centers of dissent and cultural and political upheavals, as did the regimes of the Middle East during the 15th century.

With the death and demise of the Communist State and a new view of the value of leisure, the 1980's and 90's brought a surge of interest in the coffeehouse worldwide. A new energy was infused into the old traditional coffeehouses, while numerous new ones were being opened. Today the past is still alive. Once again one can find an atmosphere of comfort and relaxation in many of the historic coffeehouses of Vienna, Budapest and Prague.

To the romance and revival of the coffeehouse!

VIENNA

# VIENNA

Vienna, the Jewel in the Crown of the old Austro-Hungarian Empire, is a city where the gilded glories of an imperial past are uniquely relevant to its vibrant present. One can almost hear the enchanting strains of Beethoven symphonies and Strauss waltzes while strolling along streets marked with Baroque architecture reflecting the wealth, power and political intrigue that once reined over the Empire.

While Vienna is no longer the seat of an empire, its sacred coffeehouses have transcended time, endured change and remain the soul of Viennese life. It is a culture; a way of life. The Viennese know that they can always find peace and solace from everyday stress in their beloved coffeehouses.

From the elegant to the bohemian to the contemporary, all share a commonality, the coffeehouse culture. Generations of people from all walks of life wile away the time contemplating life, arguing politics, reading newspapers, playing chess or cards or simply people watching. A tacit understanding exists between patron and proprietor that allows one to linger over coffee without feeling rushed or unwelcome.

The romance of the Viennese coffeehouse can trace its roots back to the Ottoman Turkish siege of the city in 1683. Vienna was on the verge of capitulation when the army reserves led by Duke Charles of Loraine and King Jan III Sobieski of Poland came to the rescue and surrounded the Turkish camp. Taken by surprise and overwhelmed by the Viennese army, the Turks fled, abandoning their belongings which included bread rolls shaped like an Islamic crescent moon, known as croissants to most or kipferl to the Viennese. Sacks of olive colored beans, which were initially mistaken as camel fodder because of their unpleasant taste, were also left behind. The camel fodder was actually unroasted coffee beans.

Georg Franz Kolschitzky, a Polish trader and interpreter who was able to cross through Turkish lines, provided intelligence and communication to the Viennese forces. After the siege, the city leaders in gratitude for his services, granted his request for the "camel fodder". He was the first to introduce coffee drinking to the people of Vienna.

The origin of the coffeehouse in Vienna is somewhat vague. However, according to Vienna history, Johannes Diodato, an Armenian trader opened the first Viennese coffeehouse in 1685 near St. Stephen's Cathedral. The Viennese quickly developed a habit for drinking the unusual hot beverage called coffee. By the eighteenth century the Viennese coffeehouse had developed a political, literary and social energy of its own, an influence for which it is well known.

During the ensuing years, many important events occurred to enhance the status of Vienna including hosting the Congress of Vienna (1814-1815) which established the new boundaries of Europe.

The status of coffeehouses also changed and began to take on a more significant role in the Viennese culture. The décor became more elaborate and comfortable, and for many Viennese it was used both as a workplace and often as a mailing address. The coffeehouse was akin to a spirited club where wits were challenged and sages shared their wisdom.

There are hundreds of coffeehouses throughout Vienna. Many have an interesting history, such as the Frauenhuber, where Mozart made appearances and much later where Beethoven played his symphonies to friends. The Dommayer is where Strauss wrote and played many waltzes. Sigmund Freud and Alfred Adler imparted their genius from the Landtmann. The Russian émigré, Leon Trotsky, played chess with Stalin and later planned the Russian Revolution of 1917 at the Cafe Central. In more recent times, WWII intrigues are well known to have occurred within the bohemian atmosphere of Cafe Hawelka, perhaps one of the last of its kind and one of the most popular, attracting patrons from the world over. The guest book at the elegant Café Demel, which once supplied delicacies to the imperial court, also includes the names of world leaders and celebrities such as Presidents Kennedy and Carter, and the Royals of England. The Café Griensteidl was considered the literary Mecca during the 19th century. Today it offers a selection of international newspapers for leisure reading while its patrons sip black coffee *mit schlag* (with whipped cream).

Although the Viennese coffeehouse has experienced change and economic hardship through the years, the romance of the Viennese coffeehouse lives on, for it is an institution with an indescribable spirit, and is the soul of Viennese life.

## Cafe Alt Wien

Backerstrasse 9
Hours: Sun-Thu 10-2 am, Fri-Sat 10-4am.

During the day, one can choose to occupy the time with newspapers and magazines, domestic and foreign, or a game of billiards. For those with a nocturnal bent, this coffeehouse comes alive after dark The well-worn terra cotta floor is an indication of its popularity. Long red velvet booths with black glass top tables grace the front room, while red vinyl is used for the back room which has gleaming white marble tabletops. Less formal than most others, coffee is served without the tray and standard small glass of water, and a corner bar displays the bottles of liqueur, which is sometimes preferred to coffee.

Cafe Bräunerhof
Stallburgasse 2
Hours: Sun-Sat 7:30 am-7:30 pm

This quaintly furnished coffeehouse with traditional desserts can be found among the antique shops on one of Vienna's smaller streets. The charm of this one room cafe is its walls and ceiling burnished by years of smoke. Resident musicians play every Saturday and Sunday afternoon while guests sit quietly reading or chatting as the sounds of piano, cello and violin swirl around them. Surrounded by an interesting collection of art, splendid music and of course, a delicious cup of coffee, the Cafe Bräunerhof allows for time well spent.

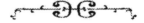

Cafe Central
Herrengasse 14
Hours: Mon-Sat 8am-10pm
       Closed Sun and holidays

The Central is imposing with its elegant interior. Its vaulted ceiling covered with colorful mosaics and beautiful hanging brass lamps, and numerous marble columns, is in the Palais Ferstel which was originally built as a stock exchange. It is where Leon Trotsky is said to have planned the Russian Revolution. The list of *who's who* included architect Adolf Loos, psycho-analyst Alfred Adler, writers Polgar, Musil, Schnitzler, and Werfel, all habitués with their own table. Although the intellectual atmosphere has waned, poets and artists continue to patronize as they did in the past. The Cafe Central also attracts politicians, businessmen and patrons who linger and enjoy the afternoon concerts of traditional Viennese music and/or listen to popular and classical selections by a performing pianist in the cafe.

As a reminder of Central's historic reputation as a literary cafe, which at one time carried 250 different newspapers daily, one can still spend time browsing through the vast selection of foreign magazines and newspapers. However, it is Central's exquisite and vast selection of pastries and coffees that is its real treasure, especially the crisp and flaky apfelstrudel. Nearly 1000 cups of coffee are served daily including special coffees with liquor. A menu of Viennese specialties is also available to those patrons preferring a more substantial fare. The Central allows its guests to recall past glories while enjoying the pleasures of the present.

Cafe Demel
Kohlmarkt, 14
Hours: Daily 10am-7pm

A designated historic landmark, the Demel is poised just steps away from Hofburg Palace. Its interior is wrapped in velvet, paneled in mahogany and dazzled by polished brass and crystal chandeliers. It's not only the old world elegance which is a feast for the eyes, its pastry is luscious and its petite sandwiches a light treat. This may explain why the Demel had been the official confectioner and caterer to the imperial court for at least 200 years.

Waitresses in long black dresses and white collars are attentive to every tidbit ready to be consumed, much as they have over the centuries. Serving a guest list which has included Beethovan, Prince Metternich, Emperor Franz Josef, Lenin, and more recently Queen Elizabeth II, Henry Kissinger, and Presidents Kennedy, Nixon and Carter is its tradition.

Cafe Diglas
Wollzeile 10
Hours: Sun-Wed 7am-11pm, Thu-Sat 7-1am

Near St. Stephan's Church and Stephansplatz, the Diglas is a conventional Viennese cafe with excellent pastries and specialties. Opened in 1923, its charming ambiance is conducive to lingering as can be seen with elderly Viennese women playing cards.

The coffeehouse was established in 1923 by Hans Diglas, the grandfather of the present owner. After WWII the cafe was made smaller and turned into an espresso bar. Its present owner, Hans Diglas III, renovated the coffeehouse in the traditional style and expanded its original size in 1988, adding a full menu to include Viennese favorites such as vegetable strudel and stuffed peppers.

The effect of the renovation is a warm and lovely interior with narrow red velvet booths and a uniquely crafted marble floor. Guests are encouraged to enjoy the atmosphere and the delicious menu for as long as they wish. The Diglas remains open year-round including holidays.

Café Dommayer
Auhofstrasse 2
Hours: Daily 7 am-midnight

Among the famous who frequented Cafe Dommayer was Johann Strauss Jr., who in 1844 made his debut as a violinist in the Cafe and earned the title of "Waltz King." Enhanced by its location in the tree-lined area just west of the Shönbrunn Palace, the Dommayer was an important venue during the height of 19th century Viennese social life. With music, dancing and, of course, delicious food and drink, one can easily visualize the glory days of the "Waltz".

A coffeehouse first appeared on this site in 1787 and in 1823 a young comb maker by the name of Dommayer became the new owner, expanding the building complex. Dommayer died in 1859, thus ending the glorious days of this special coffeehouse. The original building was demolished in 1908. It was rebuilt to its original splendor on the same site in 1935, where it stands today. It is old elegance, somewhat worn, but retaining tradition and character in its appointment and service. Once a month music swirls as concerts are held in the lovely garden during the warm months or indoors during the winter.

Cafe Frauenhuber
Himmelpfortgasse 6
Hours: Daily 8-midnight, Sun and holidays 10-10

This cafe has an interesting history. Baroque in style and built in 1720, it opened as a restaurant in 1788. Entertainment was provided and during the first year of its opening Mozart made an appearance and played a piece by Handel. In 1797 another great, Beethoven, introduced himself and performed a quintet for piano and wind instruments. Of course, Mozart and Beethovan are gone but their music remains, as well as the cafe which is the oldest existing coffeehouse in Vienna. It was opened as a coffeehouse in 1824 by a Hungarian, Alois Hánisch, as Café Herzog.
The name Frauenhuber traces back to 1891 with the purchase of the cafe by Josef Frauenhuber. It was frequented by the nearby employees of the government and military, and remains popular today

with government officials, journalists and patrons who still appreciate its history and delicious strudels. The décor includes large comfortable booths with white marble tables. Crystal chandeliers hang from the curves of the barrel vaulted ceiling.

Cafe Griensteidl
Michaelerplatz 2
Hours: Daily 8am-midnight

Location and atmosphere are its assets. The arched windows accented with red velvet draperies overlook the Hofburg and Michaelerplatz. The interior surroundings reflect its subdued elegance with white walls and dark stained paneling. The original building was demolished in 1897 during Vienna's period of renovation and rebuilding. It was rebuilt and restored to its old world charm in 1990. Considered a literary

Mecca in the late 19th century, much work was accomplished in this Cafe. Many of the Richard Strauss operas were written here as well as the Theodore Hertzel draft for the manifesto and platform for the Zionist movement and the Jewish State (Der Judenstaat). The view of the Hofburg is fantastic. The atmosphere is a reminder of the past. The desserts prepared by the Demel are superb.

Cafe Hawelka
Dorotheergasse 6
Hours: Daily-8-2am

Cafe Hawelka is the antithesis of many of Vienna's glittering and luxurious coffeehouses and deserves special mention. Established more than 50 years ago by the Hawelka's, it has become an institution alive with Vienna's recent history and is notable for its resistance to renovation. One of Vienna's most bohemian cafes, an intellectual and literary salon, it is always overflowing with patrons regardless of the hour of the day or evening. Every generation is represented: old couples, young lovers, students, artists, politicians and tourists. The seediness of its interior reflects the character of the place and the generations who have left their presence. The smoky atmosphere envelopes a melange of furniture and walls covered with posters and paintings often acquired from artists who paid for their food and coffee in kind.

Most are unaware that the coffeehouse, and the Hawelka's in particular, played a very important role in providing a haven of comfort from the WWII bleakness and devastation. The Viennese often left their bombed-out tenements and gathered at Hawelka's for warmth and shelter and to make a deal for necessary items. It is often said that the reconstruction of Austria after the war took place mostly in the coffeehouses through illicit bargaining and dealing.

Tucked away just one block from Graben, the chic and trendy pedestrian mall, Hawelka's waiters in their natty tuxedoes negotiate with the patrons, offering their superb coffee and accompaniments, and hundreds of newspapers from the continent and abroad for their indulgence. Hawelka's holds a record of longevity because of the atmosphere created by the personal touch of the Hawelka family. While Frau Josefine Hawelka prepares the coffee in the tiny kitchen, Herr

Leopold, her husband of 60 years, bustles about with a twinkle in his eye welcoming and charming his guests. The loyal patrons of this coffeehouse won't let the Hawelka's renovate or update anything; change would erase the memory of their past. And what a good thing, for the visitor has the opportunity to experience one of the most unique and historic coffeehouses of Vienna. An unforgettable experience.

## Cafe Jelinek
Otto-Bauer-Gasse 5
Hours: Mon-Fri 8am-8pm

The plaque on the wall reads "We do not cater to people in a hurry." Once inside, it is easy to understand why its blend of regular patrons linger for hours. Established in the early 1900's, it is about the size of a living room and the decor is somewhat worn with green velvet booths lining the room. The beautiful stove creates a cozy feeling of a home away from home. Students, artists, actors and intellectuals peruse the stacks of magazines and newspapers while enjoying melange or cappuccino. Delicious cakes, (the apricot cheesecake is a favorite) and twenty-two types of coffee are also served.

The proprietors since 1988 are the gracious and hospitable Herr Günter and Frau Maria, who not only extend a warm welcome but encourage their guests to stay as long as they wish. While Herr Günter prepares the coffee, desserts and various selections from the menu, the attentive Frau Maria keeps the house in order while greeting and serving her guests, many of whom she knows on a first name basis.

Cafe Korb
Brandsträtte 9
Hours: Daily 7am-midnight

More than a coffeehouse, the Korb attracts both local business people and refined elderly ladies. The gleaming white walls are complimented by dark wood and green velvet booths. Sunlight streams through its laced trim windows, and in the evening it is aglow from the light of the crystal chandeliers. The Korb is located on the corner of a narrow street in the heart of the business district where, during the Middle Ages, cloth merchants displayed and sold their goods in the square out front. Today, the carefully arranged seating for outdoor dining compliments the graciousness of the Cafe. Whether indoors or outdoors, careful attention to the comfort of the guests is reflected in the crisply appointed tables and the efficient and personal service of the waiters. It is Viennese tradition at its finest.

Cafe im KunstHaus
Weifgerberlände 14
Hours: Daily 10am-midnight

The KunstHaus is a must. It is popular with the youth of Vienna and tourists who also flock to this unique cafe to escape into a bit of fantasy. The building was designed by the artist Hundertwasser to show his works and love of nature. It is part of a museum and gift shop, and features no straight lines including uneven floors and crooked windows. The museum design is not the only attraction. The coffeehouse, which is located in the back of the building resembles a greenhouse with plants and flowers engulfing the room, and the charming outdoor patio is laden with flower baskets. The food is of fine quality, yet inexpensive, and the apfelstrudel scrumptious with grated apple and spices.

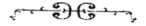

Cafe Landtmann
Dr. Karl Leugerring 4
Hours: Daily 8am-midnight

This grand old cafe is where Freud energized himself by
taking his morning coffee and discussing the issues of the
day, and where Emperor Franz Josef left his horse at its
stable while attending a performance at the theater. Today,
as in the past, the atmosphere is filled with an energy which
is still inviting to the intellectuals, journalists, government
officials and stars from the nearby Burgtheater. Contributing
to the atmosphere are people of all ages who come especially
for coffee and pastry. Viennese matrons enjoy treating
themselves to the delicious cakes every afternoon.

The Landtmann opened in 1873, when the surrounding
neighborhood was being expanded to include the new
Parliament Building, City Hall, University and Burgtheater.
Its interior maintains a 1920's flare with a gracious
atmosphere which commands proper decorum. A full menu
is available if desired as well as an outdoor terrace or
schanigartin during the summer months.

Cafe Mozart
Albertinaplatz 2
Hours: Daily 8am-midnight

Location and fine food is the attraction of the Mozart. Once the setting for a scene in the movie "Third Man", which depicted the Cafe Mozart as a dive frequented by racketeers and unsavory characters, the Cafe Mozart in reality is a luxurious coffeehouse.

In close proximity to the Opera House, its surroundings are welcoming with an interior of wood paneled walls and crystal chandeliers and the spacious scharnigarten in front to greet you. The marvelous menu includes coffee and pastries provided by the Querfeld family, owners of the famous Cafe Landtmann.

Cafe Museum
Albertinaplatz 2
Hours: Daily 8am-midnight

Architect Adolph Loos made a conscious effort toward simplicity in the first major design of his career. It was accomplished in the Museum which opened in 1899. Stark in comparison to the many ornate buildings undergoing construction in Vienna at the time, its uniqueness and plain L-shaped interior attracted the talent of the day, among them architects Otto Wagner and Josef Hoffmann, artists Gustav Klimt and Egon Schiele.

The simplicity of the interior has since evolved into a well-worn, smoke filled coffeehouse, and the guests are far more eclectic. Serious artists, writers and students have found an oasis where they can contemplate and create. Waiters move efficiently among the guests serving a variety of coffees, including coffee topped with whipped cream and served with a small glass of rum on the side.

Peter's Operncafe Hartauer
Riemergasse 9
Hours: Mon-Fri 8-2am, Sat 5-2, closed Sun

For fans of the opera, it's the Hartauer. For those who are not keen on opera, you will find the ambiance so inviting that you will remain longer than anticipated. This unique coffeehouse holds many memories. The walls are covered with photographs of the divas and opera stars who have visited since the owner, Peter Jansky, an opera officiendo, opened the coffeehouse in 1981. Notable patrons include tenor José Carreras and conductor Leonard Bernstein. A visit here makes for a relaxed mood with soft music, amicable conversation and perhaps an encounter with one of the opera stars.

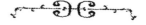

Cafe Sacher
Philharmonikerstrabe 4
Hours: Daily 6:30am-1130pm

Imperial tradition appropriately describes the Hotel Sacher Cafe. Located across the street from the State Opera House, it stands poised to greet its guests as if they were the aristocrats and royalty of years past. Upon entering into the opulence of its deep red interior and chairs gilded with gold, patrons are seated by attentive waiters, eager to pamper.

Of course it is the famous Sachertorte, which draws many to the cafe and one would be remiss not to indulge themselves in a taste of this rich yet light chocolate delight as Prince Metternich once did. The recipe for the world famous torte remains a secret since 1832 when a young apprentice cook, Franz Sacher, created the recipe especially for the Prince to enjoy.

Sacher advanced himself in the culinary world, and after the revolution of 1848, he established a delicatessen near St. Stephen's Cathedral. His son, Eduard, opened a new delicatessen in 1876 in a vacant building and converted the upper floors into the Hotel Sacher. Eduard's wife, Frau Anna, was responsible for the success of the hotel, whose list of clientele included the elite of Europe. Its private dining rooms were also an attraction for a discreet rendezvous between a gentleman and his mistress.

The Sacher is an experience surrounded by history. Today's guests can still enjoy the opulence and intrigue, real or imagined, and watch the world go by.

Schönbrunn Palace Cafes
Hours: Gloriette  Daily 8am-one hour before park
      closing
Kaiserpavillion  Daily 9am to sunset
Meierei  Daily 8am-one hour before park closing

The Schönbrunn is as much a symbol of Vienna as the coffeehouses, and the castle has three: the Gloriette, Meierei and Kaiserpavillion.  The most exquisite, the Gloriette, was built by Empress Maria Theresa as a monument in celebration of Austria's military victory over Friedrich the Great at Kolin in 1757. The setting is breathtaking with a view of the castle, the beautiful gardens and Vienna itself. The monument was opened as a coffeehouse in 1996.

The Kaiserpavillion, is a gazebo in the zoo, or Tiergarten, where it is said that before starting off the day, Emperor Franz Josef would enjoy an early breakfast in the Gazebo. Today's visitors can also enjoy a peaceful moment and indulge themselves with coffee and a tasty piece of cake while gazing up at a stucco ceiling of painted cherubs, or they can sit on the terrace and view the animals in the zoo.

A pavilion, once built for Franz Josef, now serves as a coffeehouse. The Meierei is especially welcomed by visitors with children since there is a playground adjacent to it.

Whether it's sitting on the patio embracing the surroundings, or indoors at one of the small tables, plan on staying awhile to enjoy the relaxing experience.

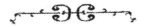

Cafe Schwarzenberg
Kärtnerring 17
Hours: Sun-Fri 7am-midnight, Sat 9-midnight

In 1887, an imperial edict was issued stating that the old city walls were to be removed and replaced by a circular boulevard lined with beautiful trees, museums, and homes for the nobility and imperial institutions. The "Ringstrasse" became Vienna's street of elegance and prestige. The Schwarzenberg, which opened in 1861, was the first coffeehouse to open on the Ring, followed by numerous other elegant coffeehouses which opened by the end of the century.

Fortunately, the Schwarzenberg has survived the wave of post-WWII demolition and in 1979, underwent extensive restoration. It is a very popular venue, especially in the summer when the sidewalk tables are arranged for your viewing pleasure. Indoors, the atmosphere is cozy with a smaller side room. For more privacy choose a window seat and gaze out the draped arched windows. In the late afternoons one can also enjoy the piano music while partaking of the usual coffeehouse offerings of coffee and deserts.

Cafe Sperl
Gumpendorferstrasse 11
Hours: Mon-Sat 7am-11pm

Under national landmark protection, Cafe Sperl is a reminder of the golden age of cafes, with its unusual interior architecture, gleaming brass chandeliers, and original Thonet chairs surrounding the marble-topped tables. It first opened in 1880, and appears unchanged except for the renovated ornate billiard tables and perhaps the more casual decorum of the patrons.

Unlike many of the other coffeehouses that dated from the turn of the century which were remodeled over the years, the Sperl's owners were not able to afford the renovation needed. When later they were financially able, they returned to the original décor, except for the chandeliers which were converted from gas to electric lights.

The owner, Herr Staub, greets his guests from an ornate counter which was once used for guests to pay their bills. As is the tradition in the Viennese cafe, he encourages one to linger over coffee without being disturbed, or to choose a game of billiards at one of the three tables.

It was composers Gustav Mahler, Franz Lehar, and the writer Franz Werfel who regularly patronized the cafe. But now, as then, it is an especially popular venue with the university students who are attracted by the reasonably priced pastries, tortes, and of course, coffees.

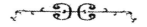

Cafe Stein
Währingerstrasse 6-8
Hours: Daily 7-2am

For the young and those who are young at heart, Cafe
Stein provides a welcoming ambiance. Close to the
University, this smoke filled cafe serves not only the
usual coffee blends and pastries, but a delicious menu
of foods including international cuisine to tempt and
satisfy the palate. Although opened in 1985, its interior
has the retro-look and color scheme of the 1960's, and
is designed to accommodate seating on several levels.
The ambiance is very appealing and each level provides
a different energy. Outdoor seating on the
Kolingstrasse is a definite consideration in summer. If
you have a need to escape reality, surf the web at one
of its internet terminals.

Cafe Weimar
Währingerstrasse 68
Hours: Sun-Tues. 8am-midnight, Wed-Sat 8-4am

In Vienna one is continually reminded of the past, owing mostly to the architecture of the 19th century and the Hapsburg Empire. The Weimar is located in a building designed by an architectural firm of that era, Feller and Helmer. The space had other uses until 1900, when it then became a coffeehouse. After WWI and several ownerships, the coffeehouse was named the Weimar in recognition of the German Weimar Republic, which in 1919 gave Germany a parliamentary democracy with a strong executive.

The present owner, Maximillian Platzer, purchased the coffeehouse in 1960 and with a slow and meticulous touch he completed the redecorating in 1992. This coffeehouse reflects tradition at its loveliest, with a high ceiling and crystal chandeliers, dark wood booths and warm hospitality to welcome its guests.

# Notes

# *Notes*

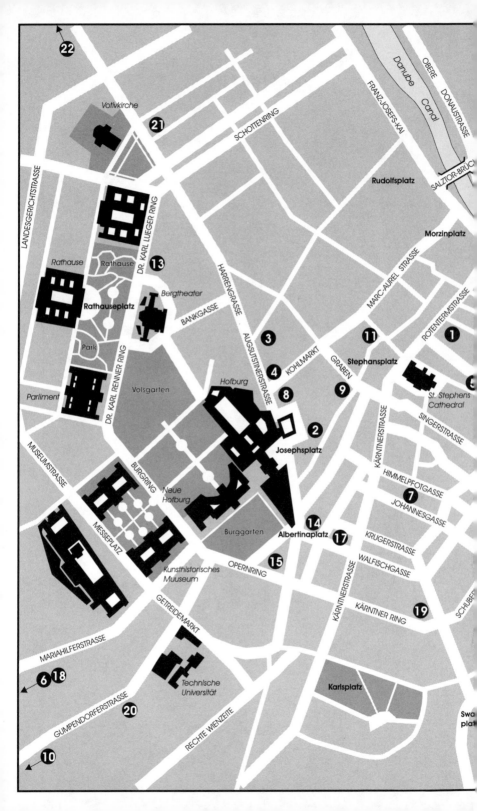

## COFFEE HOUSES

1. Alt Wein
2. Bräunerhauf
3. Central
4. Demel
5. Diglas
6. Dommayer
7. Frauenhuber
8. Griensteidl
9. Hawelka
10. Jelinek
11. Korb
12. Kunst Haus
13. Landtmann
14. Mozart
15. Museum
16. Peter's Opera Cafe
17. Sacher
18. Schönbrunn
19. Schwartzeuberg
20. Sperl
21. Stein
22. Weimer

**VIENNA**

# GREATER VIENNA

Michealerplatz Gate to Hofburg Palace

BUDAPEST

Bridge and Castle on the Danube

# BUDAPEST

Enchanting, romantic and graceful Budapest. One can immediately sense its sophistication, its legacy as a center of culture, with its exquisite opera house, palaces, government buildings, and museums. In the evening Budapest unfolds its elegance with carefully lit buildings and seven bridges which span the Danube River. The richness of Budapest's history is resplendent not only in its architecture and cultural life, but also in another important characteristic feature, the coffeehouse. While the glory days of coffeehouse society have faded as a result of political upheaval caused by Soviet tyranny and Communist corruption, as well as the ruthlessly suppressed 1956 Revolution against the regime, the spirit of the coffeehouse remains. It is evident today in the Müvesz Cukrászda, one of the oldest cafes in Budapest, and the elegant Gerbeaud. There are also numerous cafes hidden away throughout the city which are perhaps less romantic or opulent, but none the less enticing, offering their own special ambiance and character.

The history of the coffeehouse in Budapest began long before the habit of coffee drinking reached either Vienna or Paris in the late 17th century. The Ottoman Turks invading Europe had conquered the Balkans and continued northward, defeating the Hungarians at the Battle of Mohács in 1526. The entire central portion of Hungary fell into their hands. Buda was overcome in 1541 and shortly after that, the city of Pest. The remainder of Hungary was divided between the Hapsburg Empire and Transylvania.

The 150 year Turkish occupation brought with it the Turkish baths, roses, and of course coffee and the coffeehouse. For many years the coffeehouse remained characteristically Turkish, a venue where men could congregate, smoke, drink the thick Turkish coffee, known as "the black soup" in Hungarian, and conduct their business. What is considered the first uniquely Hungarian coffeehouse was opened in Buda around 1714 by a gentleman known as Blasius'. In addition to the thick smoke and pungent brew, Blasius'.included chess, card games and gambling as part of the coffeehouse activities.

While a distinctly Hungarian style and character began to develop, the coffeehouse continued to retain some of its Turkish flavor. Its ambiance held the mystique of a Turkish marketplace, at the same time providing the comfort and conviviality of a Viennese club. It was a place where one could express their Hungarian wit and enjoy the banter with fellow patrons.

Change continued to occur during the second half of the 18th century, when a coffeehouse culture developed that introduced a new way of life to many patrons who held diverse thoughts, interests and occupations. It was not unusual for the artistically inclined to mingle with the politician, or the more elite aristocrat to engage in a lively discussion with someone outside their social circle.

Among the important events in Hungarian history inspired by writers and poets, was the Revolution of 1848 against the Austrians. The famous and romantic poet, Sándor Petöfy, established his residence at the Cafe Pilváx along with the literary and political "Society of Ten", a group with Jacobin objectives. It was from this cafe that Petöfy recited his revolutionary poem, "Nemzeti dal" (national anthem) on March 15, 1848. The revolutionary demands in the "Twelve Points" were also penned in the Cafe Pilvax. Sadly, the success of this valiant revolution was short lived. Full independence was not achieved until 1920 when a supplement to the Versailles Treaty dissolved the Hapsburg Empire and granted Hungary full independence.

The coffeehouse culture reached its zenith between 1867 and WWI. At the turn of the century, Budapest was known as the city of coffeehouses. The number of coffeehouses or cafes reached nearly six hundred, and they were no longer exclusive to the artistic and the elite. There was now a coffeehouse for everyone. As their popularity grew, they began to appeal to families who wished to socialize in a respectable yet inexpensive gathering place. Correspondingly, the menu was expanded to include a wide variety of Hungarian cuisine, especially for late evening supper. At some of these coffeehouses, guests were entertained by Gypsy music.

Where at one time, salons in the homes of the aristocrats provided the venue for the intelligentsia, the coffeehouses now became the hub where intellectuals and artists held court in an atmosphere that stimulated and enriched thought and creativity. The works of the world famous composers Franz Lehár, Imre Kálmán, and Béla Bartók were often heard for the first time in the coffeehouse. The writings of Hungary's famous poets and playwrights such as the brilliant Ferenc Molnár, and the great writer of prose, Gyula Krúdy. were conceived atop the well worn tables. Architects, painters and sculptors spent endless hours sketching their dreams.

It was also the golden age for journalism and newspapers as well. An increase in literacy and a lack of any other media competition opened the market for young aspiring journalists. The coffeehouse became their club for camaraderie, work, and in many instances, their mailing address.

The decor of some of the coffeehouses became more luxurious with gilt mirrors and glittering chandeliers. The semi-palatial Cafe New York, built in 1894 and designed by the famous architect Alajos Hauszmann (who was also responsible for overseeing the reconstruction of the Royal Palace), attracted the bourgeoisie and others of like mind. However, there was also space for intellectuals and artists, and by the 1920's aspiring young actors and actresses gathered at the New York hoping to be noticed by the visiting Hollywood moguls. The New York remains a special point of interest, especially for its Art-Nouveau décor.

There were other popular coffeehouses located on Andrássy Utca, the Champ-Elysées of Budapest. Today a plaque appears on the various buildings in recognition of the former coffeehouses and their many famous patrons, especially those of the creative world.

Throughout the 1930's the coffeehouse continued to provide an atmosphere of congeniality and comfort which lasted until the Soviet Communist rule in 1945. Under Communism, many coffeehouses were closed for fear that they would become the center for revolutionary thinking. After the free elections of 1990 and the victory of the democratic opposition, a new middle class emerged and with it a generation of young Hungarians who are returning to the culture of the coffeehouse. Nostalgia for the legendary Hungarian coffeehouse lingers, a yearning for a way of life, a sanctuary where Hungarians can express their zest for learning and creativity and allow their spirits to flourish once again.

Cafe Anna
Váci utca 7
Hours: Daily 8:30 am -midnight

Originally a coffeehouse, Anna's became more of an espresso cafe after WWII. As a result of renovation, Anna's has evolved into a much more "refined" cafe where one can savor the coffee produced exclusively for Cafe Anna, either in its comfortable salon or while relaxing on the terrace facing the famous Vaci Utza.

Cafe Angelika
Bátthyany tér. 7
Hours: Daily 10am-8pm

Tucked away from the bustle of the street, the Angelika can easily be missed. With the Danube River flowing nearby, one can experience its old world charm under red and white striped umbrellas on the terrace. Or, wander inside to relax under the arches while enjoying coffee, pastries or perhaps even a glass of wine.

Central Kávéház
Károlyi Mihaly utca 9
Hours: Open 24 hours

This cafe is open to the world with vast windows that allow daylight to flood in. At night it reciprocates with a friendly glow from within.

The Central was founded in 1887 and its name is significant because it is, in fact, in the center of Budapest surrounded by cultural institutions. Once a thriving cafe, reaching the height of popularity in 1905, it fell into disrepair and was closed in 1949. It reopened in 1990 as a casino. The present owner returned it to its old world charm in 1997. Large, and situated on a corner, its windows provide a wonderful view whether you are seated directly at the window or at one of the strategically placed tables or booths. A stairway leads to a balcony which is used for special parties or for the overflow crowd A point of interest is the exquisite rosette frescoes on the ceiling.

Artists, journalists, actors, and professors are among the regulars who enjoy the substantial menu offered or the fine pastries and coffee. The Central should not be missed.

Coquan's Babkávéház
Ráday utca 15
Hours: Daily 9am-6pm

More of a coffee bar than a cafe, the Coquan's offers a vast selection of coffees including "American" in any one of its three locations. You may drink your coffee at a table or decide to carry-out your packaged choice. Whatever your mood, the Coquan's offers atmosphere and the possibility to savor a cup of its many exotic blends of coffee. Coquan's on the Ráday utca, one of three locations, is in an interesting area which is now the focus of gentrification.

Gerbeaud
Vörösmarty tér.
Hours Daily: Main Hall 9am-9pm   Side-room 7am-9pm

A favorite rendezvous place for the people of Pest for generations, it is a must for visitors. The Gerbeaud, with its confectionery known the world over, is located in the heart of the city. Recognized as one of the oldest and largest cafes in Europe, it celebrated its 140th anniversary in 1998 by rejuvenating the interior and adding a rathskeller on the lower level. Its guests can enjoy the latest creations of the master confectioner in the old world atmosphere of velvet covered chairs and marble-topped tables. The large terrace, overlooking the central square of the inner district of Pest, provides a venue where one can mingle with the locals and often the rich and famous.

Cafe Károlyi
Károlyi Mihály utca 19
Hours: Daily 9am-1am

Although it is more similar to a diner than a cafe, good coffee is served along with cocktails, beer and sandwiches. Frequented by the students from the nearby universities, the place is always full of life. The music is loud and the waitresses friendly. It's a place to party rather than a locus for quiet conversation or solitude.

Cafe Kor
Sás utca 17
Hours: Daily 9am-6pm

A superb atmosphere in the heart of the city, Cafe Kor is close to the banking district and the Basilica. It is not as ostentatious as many of the traditional cafes, but the quality of service and hospitality is warm and gracious. The ambiance, with its small tables crowded together and the bustle of the servers, gives one the feel of a Parisian coffeehouse. A delightful presentation of a menu of light fare should not be overlooked.

Lukács Café
Andrássy utca 70
Hours: Daily 8am-9pm

Among the most elegant cafes in Budapest, the Lukács, which adjoins the Central European International Bank, has recently been restored. It is beautifully appointed with marble topped tables and cane-backed chairs. The elaborate detailing of the ceiling with it's stucco, gilt and magnificent chandeliers, provides a posh ambiance without being intimidating. While the atmosphere may appear somewhat sedate, one soon finds that it is conducive to lively conversation. It is also known for its menu of specialties and pastries.

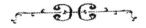

Millenium
Galeria Etterem Kavehuz
Andrassy út 76
Hours: Daily 10am-10pm

The Millenium is conveniently located between metro stops on the famous Andrássy út, the most elegant street in Budapest. Restored to its original form of 100 years ago, all of the furnishings are replicas, including the tiles on the walls which replicate the original tiles of the underground transit system. Photographs of cherished memories of Budapest fill the interior, giving the Millennium a warm and welcoming atmosphere.

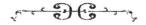

Müvész Cukrászda
Andrássy út 29
Hours: Daily 9am-midnight

One of the oldest cafes in Budapest, it has two rooms:
a non-smoking room for those who wish to be seen
through the big glass windows opening directly to
Andrassy út, and a smoky inside room to hide away
from curious eyes. Although both have antique
furniture, beautiful glass chandeliers and good service,
the inside room is more spectacular with its silky
wallpaper and huge mirror above the antique fireplace.
Tourists, students and the theater crowd mingle under
the gleaming chandeliers, nibbling at the old-fashioned
Hungarian pastries. Especially delightful are the cara-
mel topped pound cakes.

Early afternoon is the most pleasant time to drop in. It's an opportunity to mingle with the elderly *coffee-ladies* who meet their friends and spend the afternoon gossiping, drinking only one cup of coffee the entire time. Because of their presence the place is relatively smoke-free. The threadbare carpet. and marble-topped tables, over which gossip has been exchanged for generations, blends the past with the present in a most inviting way.

Cafe New York
Erzébet kärút 9-11
Hours: uncertain

The world famous New York is a special point of
interest and continues to remain open while undergoing
a prolonged renovation. Designed by the famous
Hungarian architect, Alajos Hauszmann, and built in
1894, this semi-palatial building became one of the
centers of Hungarian and Central European culture. Its
owners, an American insurance company, spared little
in their desire to create an atmosphere of space and
luxury with marble floors and columns, gold leaf,
magnificent chandeliers, and gilt mirrors. As a tribute to
its American heritage, a mural of the Statue of Liberty
and the American Flag was painted on the ceiling. On
the walls are caricatures of poets and writers who once
visited the New York and are also part of the history of
this building.

Its regular guests were writers, journalists, painters, actors and musicians, who frequently gave the coffeehouse as their postal address. Many had their own waiter and their own table. It was their home and workplace. When the turn of the century brought with it the golden age of newspapers, the editorial offices of the main newspapers of Budapest and Hungary established themselves on the upper floors of the building for the convenience of the journalists in the coffeehouse. Among the diverse patrons were members of the bourgeois as well as aspiring young actors and actresses who were frequently seen within the private alcoves. During the 1920's the New York became the focal point for Hollywood movie moguls in search of talent.

As time progressed it became increasingly less profitable to continue as a coffeehouse, so a restaurant was added in the 1930's. Life changed after WWII as well as did the New York cafe. The condition of the building began to deteriorate and its patrons, especially the journalists, were forced to move out. During the Communist era it was renamed the Cafe Hungaria for obvious reasons, but to the Hungarians it remained the New York.

Today the New York is an attraction for foreign dignitaries, royals and tourists who wish to appreciate its remarkable architecture and delicious temptations to the palate, while being serenaded by a famous Gypsy orchestra.

*Note: I have mentioned the New York because of its historic significance, but am not certain at the time of this writing that it remains open.

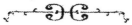

## Cafés Operett
## Nagymezö utca 19
## Hours: 11am-1am

The history of the Operett is entwined with that of one of the most famous classical theatres of the 20th century, the Operett Theater, which was established in 1922. Its location is on a street of many theatres and cafes which was once considered the Broadway of Budapest. Many of the celebrated artists of the century, writers, poets, actors and musicians gathered at the cafe either before or after performances. The Communist era was unsuccessful in closing the Operett, but it lost its glory and became more of a cafe-bar. However, the bohemian trend is becoming increasingly more visible at the Operrett, with members of Budapest's art community returning to the fold. This momentum has regained the Cafes former role among the notable cafes of Budapest.

Paris, Texas
Ráday utca 22
Hours: 10am-2pm Mon.- Fri./ 4pm-2am Sat. and Sun.

A more recent coffeehouse located on the trendy coffeehouse row on Ráday utca in Budapest, The Paris, Texas with its sidewalk cafe is a nice compliment to the other coffeehouses on the row.

Café Pierrot
Fortuna utca 14
Castle district
Hours: Daily 11am-1am

Cafe Pierrot is both a cafe and restaurant where piano music serenades its guests and often times encourages their participation in song. The 15th century building and the antique furniture within, give it an old world atmosphere. The service is quick and efficient. In addition to the coffee specialties, a menu of soups, salads and entrees are served. Since driving is prohibited in the castle district, a cab or a small BKV (Budapest transport service) bus from Moszkva tér. is advised.

Ruszwurm Cukrászda
Szentháromság tér 3
The Castle District
Hours: Daily 10am-3pm　　Closed Wednesdays

Small, and very popular. The entrance is usually crowded with guests waiting to be seated in the cozy adjoining room, which allows time for them to review the array of pastries and small sandwiches displayed in the case.

This tiny coffeehouse, dating back to 1824, was once favored for it's confectionery by the royal house of the Austro-Hungarian Empire in Vienna. It continues to offer its warm ambiance and its famous specialty, the Linzer. Once seated on the plush setees, it is easy to forget the stress of the day as time drifts away.

Cafe Verdi
Karoly körút. 1
Hours: Daily 9am-9pm

A charming cafe where locals and students come to relax and socialize. Cafe Verdi serves the least expensive coffee and largest and most inexpensive desserts of the Budapest coffeehouses. One of the three cafes owned by an American and within close proximity of each other (Cafe Mozart and Cafe Paris are the other two), it also serves sandwiches and other beverages.

# Notes

# Notes

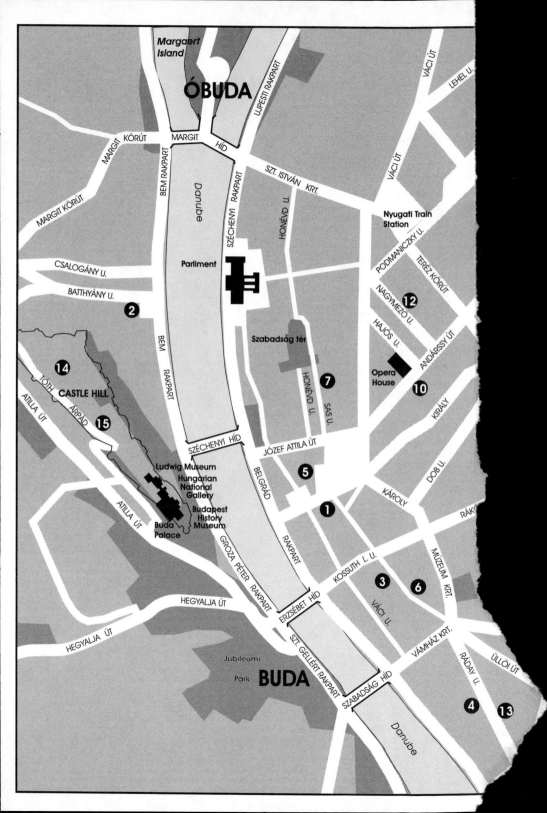

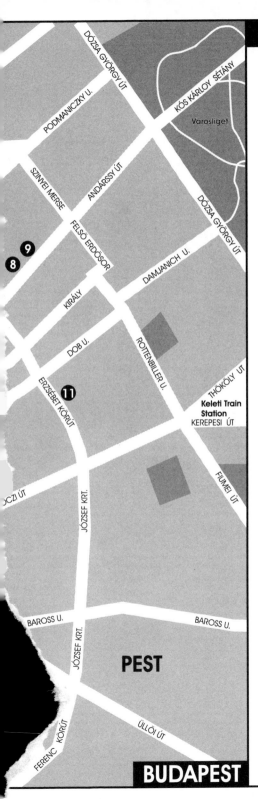

## COFFEE HOUSES

1. Anna
2. Augelika
3. Central
4. Coquan's
5. Gerbeaud
6. Károlyi
7. Kor
8. Lukács
9. Millenium
10. Müvész
11. New York
12. Operett
13. Paris, Texas
14. Pierrot
15. Ruszwurm
16. Verdi

# GREATER BUDAPEST

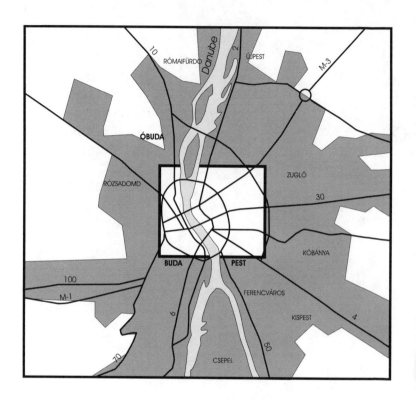

Budapest

Parliament Building on the Danube

PRAGUE

# PRAGUE

Centered in the heart of Europe and the capital of the Czech Republic, Prague is poetic, Prague is magic. High on a hill within its medieval core, the Hradcany Castle surveys the sprawling city below, brilliant in Baroque, Romanesque, and Nouveau architecture. It is a fairytale. Cobblestone streets and alleyways meander among the centuries-old buildings. Church spires and golden domes, the ancient Astronomical Clock, and the statue lined Charles Bridge, all lend to the enchantment of this city.

It is a city that has survived centuries of upheaval. In recent history, it escaped the devastation of the Second World War and endured the harshness of post-war Soviet Communism. Its embrace of capitalism after the Velvet Revolution of 1989 has led to investment in its commerce, as well as in the renovation of many of its beautiful old buildings.

The Revolution also revived an interest in the romantic coffeehouses. Although the cafe society, which at one time compared to that of Vienna or Paris, disappeared, a new enthusiasm for the cafe life has emerged. The Praguers and ex-patriots of today frequent the coffeehouses, drink coffee, smoke, and socialize, as if time was irrelevant.

According to local historians, coffee was first brought to Prague in 1703 by a Syrian, Gorgos Hatalah el Damashki, otherwise known as Jiri Deodatus, or the "Wandering Turk". A curiosity, Jiri, swathed in a turban and flowing robe, offered free samples of a most unusual brew; hot and very strong coffee.

As time evolved, the people of Prague began to develop a taste for this tantalizing beverage and Deodatus's following increased. Realizing the necessity for a coffeehouse, he opened the first in Prague in 1708 on Karlovo námesti. It became so popular that when the coffeehouse was overflowing, patrons were served outside the cafe from Prague's first outdoor cart. The original coffeehouse is gone, but a plaque marking the spot remains, "The Sign of The Golden Serpent" (buildings were differentiated by symbols rather than street numbers). Coffeehouses continued to grow in popularity and by 1841 the number in Prague had grown to forty-three.

The importance of the role that coffeehouses have played in a nation's history is especially signi-ficant in the Czech nation, particularly in Prague. They served as meeting places for patriots to vent their anger and frustration toward the oppressions of Germani-zation, and to begin organizing the Czech National

Revival. It was during the 1848 revolutions, which spread across Europe, that the movement gained momentum. In the spirit of democracy, the revisionists formed a society, meeting at the Slav Cafe (Slovanska kavarna) to plan a national program. Cafe society continued to flourish, especially after the establishment of the First Republic in 1918-19 which led to independence from Austria and the Austro-Hungarian Empire. During the 1920's and 1930's a society of artistic avant-garde formed, which included German-Jewish literary figures. Names such as the world famous poet-writer Franz Kafka and novelist Franz Werfel frequented the Narodni Kavarna. The Cafe Savoy hosted actors from Poland who performed Yiddish plays. Milena Jesenská, a journalist and lover of Kafka, was a frequent habitué of coffeehouses and wrote extensively about Prague's cafe life.

In March, 1939, the Nazi invasion brought an end to the era of Prague's coffeehouse culture. Its intelligentsia were either exterminated or forced into exile by the Nazis, thus ending a way of life as Praguers knew it to be.

After a brief postwar resurgence of the coffeehouse, the arrival of Communist tyranny in 1948 ushered in cultural constraints, which again suppressed and prevented artistic and intellectual expression. Many of the old cafes were closed for fear of dissident ideas and the activities which typically fermented in coffeehouses. For some unknown reason the Cafe Slavia was allowed to remain open, providing a venue for dissidents. Playwright and now President Vaclav Havel, writer Milan Kundera, Milos Forman, a student and later film producer, and many others met to share their thoughts and ideas about the future Velvet Revolution of 1989.

The Slavia was purchased by American developers and subsequently closed in 1991. It has since reopened along with the Cafes Imperial, Montmartre and Franz Kafka among others, all of which were closed during the Communist era.

Prague has reclaimed her cultural status in Europe, bringing with it the rebirth of the coffeehouse. The romance of the coffeehouse culture is alive once again in this quaint and magical city. The cafes and coffeehouses thrive, not only as an institution, but continue as a cradle of creativity and a barometer of national integrity in the Czech Republic.

Blatouch
Vezenská 4
Hours: Mon-Thurs noon-1am    Fri noon-2am

Wander in and stay until the midnight hour listening to jazz or soul. It is an interesting space, with a distinctive masculine ambiance and the slightest of feminine touch. One feels a sense of a Parisian cafe, which its female owners have created by furnishing it with carpets, armchairs, old bookcases and occasionally a flower or two. Among those who gather are the intellectuals, writers and expatriates who, while sharing thoughts, might consider a coffee or wine with a pleasant tasting cigar. If you are more inclined toward something a bit different to drink, you may opt for a caj (tea), either plain or with milk, honey and rum. Salads and sweets are also served as a light snack.

Damúza
Retezová 10
Hours: Mon-Fri 11am-midnight
       Sat noon-10pm, Sun noon-10pm

Damúza is the official cafe and the Czech acronym for the Academy of Dramatic Arts. Across the lane from Cafe Montmarte, students lounge in old wooden booths studying or discussing the latest issue of concern. Occasionally, theater and concert performances are held on the lower level.
Besides coffee, the menu includes beer and steak, which can also be enjoyed under a glass roof in the garden.

Ebel Coffee House
Týn 2
Hours : Daily 9am-10pm

The ultimate in brewed coffee. This small café, tucked away in an "Old Town" courtyard, is relatively new and is energized by the vitality and ingenuity of its owner, Malgarzata Ebel. She will brew coffee to satisfy your taste. She also runs a small and charming shop nearby, Vzpominsky Na Afrika, which provides the Ebel with thirty different arabica coffee beans from which she can blend coffee to your individual preferences.

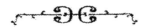

Franz Kafka Cafe
Siroká 12
Hours: Daily 10am-10pm

An old-fashioned cafe conveniently located for anyone touring the Jewish quarter. The slightly tattered lace curtains and dark wooden booths take you back in time, as do the old photographs of Kafka and life as it was lived in the old Jewish quarter. If you prefer, the convenient tables along the street provide a pleasant pause to enjoy a tasty cup of coffee.

Grand Hotel Evropa
Václavské námesti 25
Hours: Daily 9am-10pm

It is worth taking the time to stop in at Prague's legendary art nouveau hotel. The original design was the masterwork of architect Belsky. When built in 1889, it was named "The Archduke Stephan". Reputed architects, Bendelmayer, Hubschmann and Letzel, contributed with their art nouveau designs to the reconstruction of the building during the 1903-1905 period. The statues on the front were crafted by sculptor Ladislav Saloun. The interior design also reflects its remarkable architecture with lush woodwork and a unique balcony overlooking the cafe.

Because of its location in the hub of activity on Wenceslas Square, it no doubt has witnessed many historical events and changes which makes it not only an architectural treasure but a historical landmark.

Cafe Galerie
Hradcanské námesti 15
Hours: Daily 10am-6pm except Monday

The Cafe Galerie can be found in a quiet courtyard of the Stemberg Palace on the Hradcany Square. It provides a welcoming interlude of repose during your visit to the National Gallery or Prague's Castle.

The Globe Coffeehouse & Bookstore
Pstrossova 6
Hours: Daily 10am-Midnight

Although the Globe has become somewhat of an institution for expatriates, it is also a cafe for the interesting and interested as well. Offering an ambiance conducive to intimacy or socializing, this comfortable cafe and bookstore is considered the literary center of post-revolutionary Prague. It often draws those of inter-national and local literary fame to the weekly reading program. Cozy up in the reading room with a cafe-latte and a foreign newspaper or scan the shelves for authors from Europe and abroad. You may want to peruse the menu for lunch or a snack. A cafe not to be over-looked.
Internet terminals are available.

Cafe Imperial
Na porici 15
Hours: Daily 9am-1pm

Neglected for decades, the Cafe Imperial has reopened
and takes us back to what once was within the Hotel
Imperial. Built in 1914, and ranked among the most
beautiful monuments in Europe, one is immediately
struck by the art nouveau sculpted porcelain tiles on the
walls which extend up to an equally beautiful floral
mosaic-covered ceiling. The interior is the only original
one of its kind in the world. A spacious L-shaped room
with large windows overlooks the busy thoroughfare.
Besides the twenty different coffees served, liqueur and
a full menu are available. Live jazz and swing music can
be enjoyed most evenings.

Jazz Cafe
Opatovická 14
Hours: Mon-Fri 10am-11pm    Sat-Sun Noon-11pm

Excellent espresso, beer, wine, and a jazz soundtrack which plays jazz only, provides an atmosphere for a snug refuge. Smoke filled, and with an array of mismatched furniture, it is frequented by local writers, intellectuals and bohemians.
Packaged health foods are also available and you may choose a cup of tea if you prefer.
Adjoining the Cafe is a bookstore gallery.

Cafe Konvikt
Bartolomejská 11
Hours: Mon-Fri 9am-1am    Sat-Sun   Noon-1am

A must for those with a bohemian bent. Bright and airy, there's plenty of space in this cafe/pub to spend an afternoon reading or writing political works. Or enjoy the lower level surrounded by young intellectuals or lively groups of gossiping locals.

Café Louvre
Národni trida 20
Hours: 8am-11pm daily

Café Louvre, established in 1902, is the ultimate in tradition, style and individuality as is exemplified by the cream and turquoise colored interior. The cafe, with its high ceiling, occupies the second floor off of a large atrium and adjoins a swank restaurant with the same name. A special point of interest is the original Billiard Hall which is still in use.
The menu offers a variety of choices and a breakfast of substance is served on the weekend.

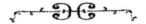

Malostranská Kavárna
Malostranské námesti 5
Hours: Daily 9am-11pm

Established in 1874 in a late eighteenth-century palace, it remains a favorite meeting place with the locals. It is a time-honored cafe that, along with the Slavia, was a hub for the opposition, and a student refuge throughout the Communist era. Today, the students from the neighboring university share tables with people of all ages and interests, all enjoying food and drinking coffee or beer.

Cafe Milena
Staromestské námestí 22
Old Town Square
Hours: Daily 10 am-10 pm

Named after Franz Kafka's secret love, Milena
Jesenska, it offers not only a fantastic view of the
Astronomical Clock in the Old Town Square, but
introduces the guest to the world of Franz Kafka.
Nestled in on the second floor, the two-room
coffeehouse is also a part of the Franz Kafka Center,
which is a non-profit organization attempting to revive
and promote awareness of the cultural plurality of the
Central European region. Cheerful and airy, guests are
able to relax either at tables or small sofas while sipping
the strong coffee, tea or selecting from a menu of
assorted delicacies. Magazines and newspapers are
available.

Cafe At Minute
Corner of the Renaissance House
Near the Clock in the Old Town Square
Hours: Daily: 10am-10pm

The first non-smoking cafe in Prague can easily be overlooked because of your fascination with the building. Tucked away on the ground floor of the Renaissance House with its ornately carved base-relief figures, Café At Minute, offers 50 types of coffee beverages and a menu with Czech cuisine. Local history indicates that Franz Kafka resided above the coffeehouse for seven years.

Charles Bridge towards Castle

Cafe Montmarte
Retezová 7
Hours: daily 10am-1am

Down a narrow lane in the old town area, this cafe is said to have an interesting if not intriguing history. It first opened on a hot summer night in 1911 and soon became the venue for Czech, Yiddish, and German artists to take the stage. Its patrons were the likes of Hasek, Kafka, Langer, Meyrink and Werfel who are believed to have wiled away the days and nights talking and drinking in the heart of intellectual life. Nearly a century after its opening, it appears as though nothing has really changed, as noted by the well-worn furnishings. As in the past, lively and stimulating conversations into the late hours continue over a marvelous cup of café au lait or perhaps something a bit stronger.

The Municipal House (Kavara Obecni Dum)
Námesti Republiky 5
(Faces the Republic Square)
Hours: daily 8am-10am

While the menu is not limited to coffee, it has one of
the most extensive coffee and pastry menus in Prague.
It serves over 1,000 coffee beverages daily, including
brewed coffees prepared from Jamaican Blue Mountain
and Maragogype beans, as well as espresso-based
beverages. However, its sumptuous and artistic setting
is conducive to lingering over something more
substantial chosen from their lengthy menu of tempting
meals, accompanied by a wine and beer list.

Opened in 1912 as a cultural center, The Municipal House is one of the most remarkable constructions of Prague Art Nouveau. It is a unique harmony of architectural and painting styles of the 19th and 20th centuries, enhanced by a wide range of decorative styles and materials, as well as high quality craftsmanship. For many years it was alive with cultural activity and its cafes were overflowing. Eventually, poor economic conditions and disrepair forced its closing. It had undergone several partial renovations, the latest was a thorough renovation taking three years and one billion Czech crowns. It reopened in May of 1997.

Cafe de Paríz
In the Hotel Pariz
U Obecniho Domu 1
Hours:  Daily  10am-11pm

Cafe de Paríz is to be enjoyed for its extraordinary ambiance.  Superbly located in the heart of Prague, and only minutes from the Old Town Square, it is in the Hotel Paríz which was built in 1904.

The center of the bohemian culture of Prague, works from artists such as Alphonse Mucha, considered the Republics best, are juxtaposed with the Art Nouveau style of the 1920's decorating. While the coffee menu is good, it is the experience of the atmosphere and sharing the moment with other guests while listening to live jazz which is memorable. Cafe de Paríz is Prague in style.

Radost FX
Belehradská 120, Praha 2
Hours: Daily 11:30 am-5am

In evidence throughout Prague is the immigrant community which has become an essential part of the coffeehouse culture. One of the most interesting ethnic groups are the Yugoslavs, who say they left the former Yugoslavia because they prefer to make love rather than war, and who are eager to share their gregarious nature in the warmth and friendliness of the eclectic FX. Amid the smoke filled rooms and well-worn furniture are the works of local artists displayed in the art gallery. The fact that the FX remains open until 5 am draws music lovers for regular evening concerts or perhaps poets for a Sunday night reading. Besides the coffee and cozy atmosphere, its vegetarian menu includes spinach burgers, pasta, soups, sandwiches and salads. Brunch on the weekend has become a ritual, and a pleasant way to spend the day.

Cafe Slavia
Smetanovo nábrezi 2
Hours: Daily 9am-11pm

The Slavia, the center of free Czech spiritual, artistic and intellectual life for centuries, has reopened after a long and painful closure. It was the hub for Czech dissidents including Vaclav Havel who plotted the overthrow of Communism and the Velvet Revolution of 1989. Its closing in 1991 was criticized by President Havel as "a criminal attack on the intellectual life of Prague." Recently reopened, the Cafe, opposite the National theater and with a fantastic view of the Prague Castle and Vltava River, reflects the 1930's spirit with its art deco fixtures, tasty menu and efficient service.
A memorable venue for reminiscing about Czech history.

Cafe Y Svatého Vojtecha
Vojtesská 14
Hours: Mon-Thurs 8am-8pm,  Fri 8am-10pm
       Sat 10am-10pm,  Sun 10am-8pm

Relax and enjoy the view of the Vlatava River through large bay windows as you sip your coffee while lost in thought. Just behind the National Theater, this small and quiet cafe attracts a diverse and sophisticated patronage of professionals, as well as the artistic and intellectuals. Daily Czech newspapers are available for your interest and pleasure.

Vzpaminsky Na Afriku

## Vzpaminsky Interior

# Notes

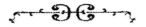

# *Notes*

# COFFEE HOUSES

1. Blatouch
2. Damúza
3. Ebel
4. Franz Kafka
5. Hotel Evropa
6. Galerie
7. Globe
8. Imperial
9. Jazz
10. Konvikt
11. Lauvre
12. Malostranska
13. Milena
14. At Minute
15. Montmarte
16. Municipal House
17. de Pariz
18. Radost
19. Slavia
20. Y Svatého
21. Vzpominsky

## PRAGUE

# GREATER PRAGUE

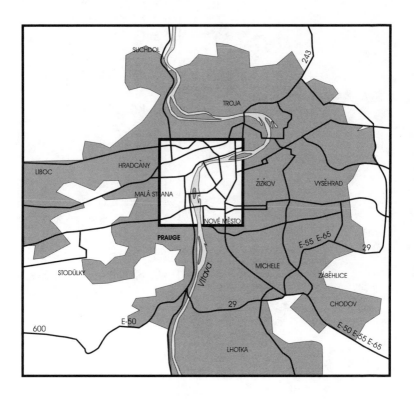

**A Detail on the Town Hall in
Prague's Jewish Quarter**

**Pharmacy Museum in Mala Strana
(The name is coincidental!)**

# Notes

# Notes

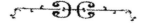

# Notes

# Notes

# Notes

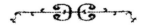

# Notes

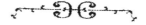

# Notes

# Notes

# Notes

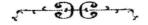

# Notes

# Notes